ON-SITE

Zondervan/Youth Specialties Books

Adventure Games
Amazing Tension Getters
Attention Grabbers for 4th–6th Graders (Get 'Em Growing)
Called to Care
The Complete Student Missions Handbook
Creative Socials and Special Events
Divorce Recovery for Teenagers
Feeding Your Forgotten Soul
Get 'Em Talking!
Good Clean Fun
Good Clean Fun, Volume 2
Great Games for 4th–6th Graders (Get 'Em Growing)
Great Ideas for Small Youth Groups
Greatest Skits on Earth
Greatest Skits on Earth, Volume 2
Growing Up in America
High School Ministry
High School TalkSheets
Holiday Ideas for Youth Groups (Revised Edition)
Hot Talks
Ideas for Social Action
Intensive Care: Helping Teenagers in Crisis
Junior High Ministry
Junior High TalkSheets
The Ministry of Nurture
On-Site: 40 On-Location Programs for Youth Groups
Option Plays
Organizing Your Youth Ministry
Play It! Great Games for Groups
Teaching the Bible Creatively
Teaching the Truth about Sex
Tension Getters
Tension Getters II
Unsung Heroes: How to Recruit and Train Volunteer Youth Workers
Up Close and Personal: How to Build Community in Your Youth Group
Youth Specialties Clip Art Book
Youth Specialties Clip Art Book, Volume 2

ON-SITE

40 ON-LOCATION YOUTH PROGRAMS

by Rick Bundschuh

Youth Specialties

ZONDERVAN PUBLISHING HOUSE
Grand Rapids, Michigan

On-Site
Copyright © 1989 by Youth Specialties

Youth Specialties Books are published by Zondervan Publishing House
Grand Rapids, Michigan 49530

Library of Congress Cataloging-in-Publication Data

Bundschuh, Rick, 1951–
   On site.

   1. Church group work with teenagers: 2. School excursions. I. Title.
BV4446.B86   1989   268′.433   88-20613
ISBN 0-310-43061-5

All Scripture quotations, unless otherwise noted, are taken from the *Holy Bible: New International Version* (North American Edition). Copyright © 1973, 1978, 1984 by the International Bible Society. Used by permission of Zondervan Bible Publishers.

Edited by David Lambert
Cover illustration by Rick Bundschuh
Interior illustrations by Tom Finley

Printed in the United States of America

92   93   94   95   96 / CH / 10   9   8   7   6   5   4   3

Dedicated to my mom,
who took me places.

ON-SITE   **Contents**

Preface **8**
Going On-Site **9**
A Greenhouse **12**
A Jail **14**
A Dump **16**
A Construction Pit **18**
A Tower **20**
A Boat **22**
An Athletic Track **24**
A Crypt **26**
A Rooftop **28**
A Garden **30**
A Cemetery **32**
A Tree **34**
A Pigpen **36**
A Narrow Path **38**
A Courtroom **40**
A Barn, Silo, or Warehouse **42**
A Wheat Field **44**
A Manure Pile **46**
A Lighthouse **48**

A Synagogue **50**
A House of Mirrors **52**
A Spring **54**
A Bank Vault **56**
A Vineyard **58**
A Polluted Pond **60**
An Armored Car **62**
A Cancer Ward **64**
A Fish Pond **66**
An Old Folks' Home **68**
A Bakery **70**
A Nursery **72**
A Dark Room **74**
An Upper Room **76**
A Potter's Workshop **78**
A Field **80**
On Center Stage **82**
A Foundation **84**
A Sheep Ranch **86**
A Beach **88**
A Fortress **90**

Preface

This is a book for people who work with kids. Its main purpose is to give creative tools to people who want to make God's Word come alive to their students.

It is my prayer that the ideas in this book, or any new ones that are sparked by it, can have eternal significance by bringing concepts of God into better focus.

I am indebted to the youth group at Kalaheo Missionary Church for being willing guinea pigs for on-site ideas, to Tom Finley for his wisdom, and to Lauren for her love and encouragement.

Rick Bundschuh
Kauai, Hawaii

INTRODUCTION   Going On-Site

Taking a group of students out for a living object lesson isn't a new idea. Jesus used the technique often as he hiked the rolling hills of Galilee. Even though centuries have passed between those first lessons recorded in the New Testament and the lessons we prepare from week to week, the benefit of going on-site hasn't diminished.

Going on-site provides students with an experience that is three dimensional, living, and far removed from a classroom setting with pencil and paper. Because they get *involved* in the lesson, students learn better and remember more. Kids may forget in a week even the best of lessons taught in the classroom, but many will remember for years a lesson that became an experience. It is these lessons, well remembered, that bring God's word home to the heart time after time.

While going on-site can be as easy as piling in the car, here are some tips to help make sure the teaching experience is a real winner!

1. CHECK THINGS OUT IN ADVANCE. Be sure to visit the site before the day you plan to take the group. Be sure to get proper permission and cooperation from individuals who run the facilities. (Unless you plan to do your lesson from the back of a squad car.)

    It's often difficult to get permission to visit some sites, such as a mortuary or jail cell. Contacts within your church or the public relations person of the organization may be able to arrange it. Smaller communities are often more flexible than larger cities, but you never know what the answer will be unless you ask.

    It's a good idea to call or write a note of confirmation a day or two before your event to jog memories. Send a thank-you note when the event is over.

    As part of your advance work, log the distance and the time it takes to get to your site, so that you allow enough time to get your lesson in before having to return to the church.

2. SET UP YOUR VEHICLES IN ADVANCE. Line up cars or a van; have them clean and filled with gas before the time of departure.

3. PREPARE HANDOUTS IN ADVANCE. As a rule, it's best to go on-site with as little paperwork or reading to do as possible—although there are some settings where sitting around with Bibles and papers works fine. Just use your common sense.

   If you do need to use some paperwork or some Scripture passages in a difficult setting, here are some suggestions: Pre-print the appropriate Scripture and make copies to distribute at the site, rather than asking the students to bring their Bibles. If writing assignments are involved, try providing clipboards.

   Remember, too, that Scripture reading and paper responses can be done in a classroom setting before or after the event.

4. TAKE A SMALL GROUP. Lessons done on-site are best done with ten or fewer students. Control is easier, and the attention of the kids is more quickly directed. Discussions and conversations are better conducted with fewer students.

   If you have a large class, have a select group go to the on-site activity and prepare a report or video presentation to show the rest of the class, or break up into small groups and go to different sites for the day.

5. ELIMINATE FIGHTS OVER SEATING. Some kids, especially junior highers, may fight over preferred seating in the vehicles, thereby starting the day off with poor attitudes. Settle this in advance with any method that works. (Our group always uses "age has priority." The oldest kid has the first choice. The younger kids hate it till they're older.)

6. KNOW YOUR STUDENTS. Know the group you are taking on-site and bring extra help if you think there may be more "energy" in the crowd than you can handle on your own.

7. ON-SITE COURTESY. Stress to your students the kind of behavior that you expect them to show before you leave the church. Make sure to let them know what is off-limits. Acknowledge with a "thanks" the assistance of anyone who helps with the project.

8. MAKE A DAY OF IT. Sometimes stopping for a milkshake after the lesson can be a great way to develop relationships with the kids in your class and to continue the learning process.

9. BE CREATIVE. By bringing along cameras, videos, or tape recorders you can stretch the learning experience or capture moments to share with others in the church.

    On-site activities can be fun, memorable, and educational. They can make a difference between a dull, lifeless lesson and one that "really goes somewhere."

    The following pages of On-site will give you suggested places to take your students as well as a lesson plan that can be followed for each of the sites.

    These lesson plans are merely ideas and suggestions, so please feel free to customize, stretch, or rework the teaching methods to the manner best suited to your lesson, your class, and your own teaching style. For example, you may find a completely different truth that can be illustrated by a site suggested in this book. Just customize your lesson to fit it!

10. ONE CONCEPT IS BEST. Some sites may suggest a number of ideas to communicate but it is generally best to tie the lesson down with one main focus or thought. Whatever that idea is, you can be sure that it will not be forgotten soon.

11. USE ON-SITE ACTIVITIES SPARINGLY. The ideas in this book can bring fun, excitement, and enthusiasm. Think of activities as seasoning to spice up an existing program, rather than a steady course.

So—those are the basic principles that will encourage successful on-site lessons. Now let's look at some suggested places to take your students and at some lesson plans that can be followed for each of the sites.

But remember: These lesson plans are merely ideas and suggestions. They'll work best if you customize, stretch, or rework them to find the approach best suited to your lesson, your class, and your own teaching style. You're limited only by your own imagination!

ON-SITE IN A GREENHOUSE

Take your students to visit a greenhouse, particularly in the middle of winter.
This is a great location to talk about the various important elements in Christian growth—for example, the right environment, food, care, and ultimate productivity. During winter, the greenhouse environment in most parts of the country is an especially stark contrast to the plant world outside.

Variations: Create a lesson around the life cycle of a plant; show the seasons of growth from a seed to a fruitful plant, all in the greenhouse of course. For extra fun, wear a Hawaiian shirt and shorts to teach this lesson (under your winter clothes, of course).

Focus: Christians grow in the right environment.
Bible passages to share and discuss: John 15:1–17, John 7:37–38, John 8:12, Hebrews 10:25.

Getting Started

Pull a packet of seeds out of your pocket and ask your students to come up with a list of things that would make the seeds grow and produce fruit.

Point out how those elements are provided in the greenhouse you are visiting.

Looking in the Word

Distribute slips of paper on which are written out the verses you want to use. Ask the students to read the passages aloud; see what similarities your group can find between the description given in the Bible and the care or needs of plants in a greenhouse.

Plugging into Daily Life

Ask your students to describe a function of some element of the greenhouse and to compare it to some way that a good spiritual environment will help us to grow as Christians. For example, Jesus claims to be water and light for us, which means we need to soak up what he has to say by reading his word and talking to him. We can expect God to "tend" us. We can keep our life from being a nesting ground for the "weeds" of sin. We can join with other Christians in church.

Contrast the world of the greenhouse with the cold winter outside, showing the difference that growing in God's loving environment can make.

Adding It All Up

Try to arrange to give each student a small plant from the greenhouse you visit. Write a passage of Scripture from today's lesson (or have the students do it) on a small card and tape it to the pot of the plant. Send it home with your students as a reminder to soak up some of God's warmth this week.

JAIL

Make arrangements to have your group incarcerated in a local jail cell. You can teach your lesson from outside of the bars while your students remain locked up, or you can join them inside.

Because people from both the Old and New Testament found themselves in prison, a jail cell can be used to teach a variety of lessons. Or, use a cell to talk about the "prison of sin" with its limited freedom to enjoy life.

Depending on the facility, you may be able to spend your whole lesson time in a cell or you may only be able to stay locked up for a few minutes. If the latter, use your time in the cell primarily to soak up the sensation of being a jailbird, then discuss your lesson at another location.

Focus: To come close to the experience of Paul and Silas in prison.
Bible passage to share and discuss: Acts 16:16–36

Getting Started

Create a phony warrant for the arrest of each of the students in your class, ordering each to appear at the time and place of your meeting. Send the warrants in the mail several days before you plan to go on-site.

Have an accomplice dressed as a judge start the meeting by sentencing each kid in the group to prison for being a member of your group. (If you have a member of your church who is a police officer, he or she might come in uniform to "arrest" each student and escort them to the "paddy wagon.")

Make sure to get some photos of your kids in jail.

Looking in the Word

While in the jail cell, share with your students the experiences of Paul and Silas, or have them read it for themselves while they are doing time.

Ask your kids to share what differences and similarities there might be between the jail that Paul and Silas found themselves in and the one the youth group is experiencing.

Ask: "Would you like to spend years in a cell like this for doing a good thing? Would it make you angry at God if you were convicted for such a meaningless crime? Why or why not?"

Plugging into Daily Life

Distribute paper and pencils to each student. Ask them to imagine that they're going to be stuck in a jail cell for an indefinite period of time for the crime of being a Christian. But the jailer tells them that if they renounce Christianity and curse Christ they can go free.

Ask each student to write a letter to a non-Christian friend explaining why they would rather stay in prison than renounce Christ.

Adding It All Up

On index cards write Paul's motto: "For to me, to live is Christ and to die is gain" (Phil. 1:21). Make one card for each student. Ask them to take their card home and memorize the verse.

Another option: Put the passage on a large placard and photograph the students holding it inside the jail cell. Make a print for each student to keep.

DUMP

For a lesson that is both visual and olfactory, take your crew to a local dump. If you plan to traipse through the garbage warn students in advance to wear grubby clothes.

Dumps provide excellent examples of what eventually happens to all the material things we treasure so much, and the contrast that a life invested in spiritual and eternal things can make. Everything in a dump used to be new and useful—but none of the things people crave last forever.

Focus: Invest your energy in things that last forever rather than things that crumble and rot.

Bible passage to share and discuss: Matthew 6:19–24.

Getting Started

Don't tell the kids where you are taking them. On your way to the dump cruise by some really nice parts of town or by the local Porsche dealer. Drive slowly and let the kids take a good look at all the expensive houses and shiny cars.

Ask your students to share what their latest purchases have been or what they plan to spend their money on in the near future.

Looking in the Word

When you reach the dump, share Matthew 6:19 with your students. Ask them to point out things that might have been treasures to somebody at one time that are now just useless junk.

Plugging into Daily Life

As you sit on piles of rubbish (or if you can't stand the smell, on the outskirts of the dump), ask your students to help you compile a list of things that would never find their way to a dump (or cemetery—the "dump" for humans). Try to get kids to isolate specific thoughts and actions that are eternal in nature, such as doing a kind thing for the "geek" of the school or getting to know God better. Jot down on a piece of paper what your kids say.

Adding It All Up

At a convenient time or location distribute pencils and paper and have your students write down one thing they will invest in this week that can have eternal consequences. Do not ask kids to share this with anyone since it's between themselves and God.

CONSTRUCTION PIT

F ind a pit large enough to put your group into and deep enough that they won't be able to climb out. Bring a ladder with you so that the kids can get down into the pit, and then pull the ladder out so that you can sit above your captive audience. The idea is for them to share the emotions that Joseph must have felt while being put in the cistern by his brothers.

Needless to say, don't stick your kids in any kind of dangerous hole. Be sure to get permission to use the site.

Focus: A graphic identification with the experience of young Joseph.

Bible passage to share and discuss: Genesis 37.

Getting Started

Driving to the site, ask your students: "Have any of you ever been so mad at your brother of sister that you did or almost did something you regretted?" Encourage them to share specific incidents. Explain that today they are going to hear an example from Scripture of the same kind of feelings.

Looking in the Word

After you have lowered your class into the pit, simply retell the story of Joseph, his coat, and his betrayal by his brothers.

Ask kids to share how they might have felt if their brothers had done something like this to them.

Ask students to share what they would have done if they were in Reuben's shoes. Would they squeal to dad? Why or why not?

Plugging into Daily Life

After you have brought your students out of the pit, ask them to think of ways that a person could be isolated, betrayed, or sold out by their friends, or even Christian brothers. Have them give examples (or be ready to share some of your own ideas).

Ask:

1. How can a group of students "shut out" someone they don't want to join them?

2. If you were a Christian member of a group that was doing this, what would be your response to the "shut out" person? To the group?

Adding It All Up

Ask your class to think of one person who is getting the isolation treatment at school, church, or the neighborhood. Ask them to silently commit to making that person feel cared for.

TOWER

Most towns, even in the flattest of terrains, have a tower that can be reached by stairs. Many old churches, for instance, have a belfry. From this vantage point a small class not only has a great view but can get a visual picture of one aspect of the temptation of Christ.

Make sure the tower will be open when you want to use it, or make special arrangements to be allowed up on a rooftop.

Focus: Getting a better idea of the temptation of Christ.
Bible passages to share and discuss: Luke 4:1–13, 1 Corinthians 10:11–13.

Getting Started

From your lookout on the top of the tower, ask your students questions such as: "How much money would it take for you to jump off this tower? How about onto a net? With a bungie cord strapped to your leg? With a parachute?"

Point out that the reason the group is up on the tower today is to discuss a situation in which Christ was challenged to jump from such a height, and to see his response to that challenge.

Looking in the Word

Divide the verses of Luke 4:1–13 among your students and have them read about the event. Or simply explain to your class what occurred in this passage.

Invite your students to figure out what three areas of temptation Satan tried to use on Christ. (Physical temptation: Christ was hungry. Material temptation: The wealth and splendor of the world. Mental temptation: He tried to make Jesus prove himself.)

Plugging into Daily Life

Distribute paper and pencils. Ask your students to work in pairs to make a list of temptations that would be common to the average high school student. Have your class members share their answers.

Point out which of the temptations are most mentioned.

Ask your students: "How did Jesus resist temptation? What are ways we can resist temptation? What help does 1 Corinthians 10:11–13 give to Christians today?"

Adding It All Up

Pass out small sheets of paper and instruct your students to write down a temptation that they often face.

Then have your students fold their papers into airplanes and symbolically send Satan's influence away from their lives by sailing the gliders off the tower.

ON-SITE IN A   BOAT

Arrange to go sailing in a small boat and sail on a bay or lake near your church. Make sure the boat will be waiting for you at the water's edge, and let the kids know in advance not to wear their Sunday best.

While in the middle of the lake lead a Bible study about Jesus walking on the water while the disciples sat terrified in their boat.

Variation: Use the boat to cross a lake where you have a breakfast prepared on the beach (see page 88) as a visual lesson about John 21.

Focus: We need to put our complete trust in Christ no matter what the circumstances.
Bible passage to share and discuss: Matthew 14:22–32.

Getting Started

On the way to the water, ask your students to define the word "miracle." After a number of students have given their definition, share with them that a miracle is an event that goes beyond or contradicts the known laws of nature. As you get to your boat tell your students that the group is going to try to sense the intensity of a miracle that the Lord performed for his disciples.

Looking in the Word

As soon as the boat reaches the center of the lake or bay, read to your students Matthew 14:22–32. Spark a discussion by asking questions such as:

1. Do you think the reaction of the disciples when they first spotted Jesus was warranted?

2. Do you think Peter made his comment out of fear, stupidity, or faith?

3. What caused Peter to sink?

4. Do you think Jesus was hard on Peter? Why or why not?

5. What kind of circumstances sink Christians today?

Plugging into Daily Life

On your return trip, ask your group to create new words for "Row, Row, Row Your Boat" that might reflect things a Christian could learn from the incident just studied. For example: "Faith, Faith, keep your faith when the waves are high . . . "

Suggestion: Use a portable tape recorder to tape the final version of the song on the way back to the church.

Adding It All Up

Back where it's warm and dry, ask your students to complete the following sentence and be prepared to share what they have written: "One thing I learned on our boat ride was . . . "

ATHLETIC TRACK

A simple but effective way to bring to life the biblical idea about "running the race" is to take your group to a local track and conduct your study on the grass near the finish line.

If you plan to sit in the field, make sure that there won't be a meet going on. (If there is, you can always conduct your class in the upper bleachers.)

Note: Some tracks are very busy places. To avoid distractions, it is usually best to find a field that's seldom used by the general public.

Focus: We are to put our effort and energy into running the race of life for Christ.

Bible passages to share and discuss: Hebrews 12:1–3, 1 Corinthians 9:24–27.

Getting Started

Invite your students to line up on a starting line and run a 25-yard dash against each other (or you).

Talk to your class about the difference between running a sprint and running a distance race. Ask them what they would do differently.

Looking in the Word

Sitting on or near the track, invite your students to examine the Scripture that paints a picture of the Christian life as a race. Ask them:

1. What does the race represent?
2. What do we get if we win the race?
3. What must we do to ourselves to win this race?

Plugging into Daily Life

Give each student an index card or a piece of paper and ask them to write down one thing that can tangle up a high school student trying to win the race for Christ. Have the students pass the cards to their right and add another *different* idea to the card they receive. Continue until the cards have gone in a full circle. Ask students to read the contents of their cards.

Adding It All Up

Ask your students to commit to a particular discipline for the week to help get them in shape to run the Christian race with endurance. It could be reading a particular book of the Bible, making a special prayer time, or spending time being quiet and thinking about God each day; encourage them to choose something especially appropriate and helpful for them.

Even though they're uncommon in some parts of the country, a little scouting around can often find a cemetery with an above-ground crypt or tomb.

The door to the tomb will probably be locked, but a study on the raising of Lazarus can be conducted right outside the door. From there, kids can get a limited sense of the terror that must have come over the observers when Christ called Lazarus out of the tomb.

Focus: Christ is the one who give us the hope of a resurrection.
Bible passage to share and discuss: John 11:1–44.

Getting Started

When you arrive at the cemetery, wander around the tomb you'll be using. Explain the function of a family tomb and how they are similar to tombs used thousands of years ago.

Looking in the Word

While at the cemetery, divide the passage into several parts and assign each person in your group at least one section to read. Ask them to explain to the others in the group what occurred in their part of the Scripture.

Ask questions such as:

1. Suppose a person were to emerge from *this* tomb. What would your reaction be?

2. What do you think people thought of Christ after this miracle?

3. What hope does that demonstration of power give to those of us who are alive and those who already lie in these graves?

Plugging into Daily Life

Ask your students to imagine that they have a friend who picked up the disease AIDS through a blood transfusion. This friend is now on the critical list and has very little time left to live. Distribute paper and ask the class to write a letter of hope to this friend based on what they have considered here at the crypt.

Adding It All Up

Ask your students to meditate quietly about Christ's resurrection from the dead for a few minutes and then be prepared to share with the group one word that expresses the thoughts that came to them. (For example, a student may just respond with the word "powerful" or "hopeful.") Close in a prayer of thanksgiving for Christ's promise of resurrection for us.

ROOFTOP

With a little cooperation from a home owner in your church, your group can reconsider one of the most interesting miracles recorded in the New Testament: the healing of the paralytic man.

A roof with very little slope is the best location for this lesson. (Otherwise kids keep falling off the roof and making a mess on the sidewalk.) Also, keep the group size small so not to put too much weight on the roof.

But remember not to let the kids dig through the roof—some biblical examples should be taken only so far.

Focus: No obstacle is too great to bring your friends to Jesus.

Bible passage to share and discuss: Mark 2:1–12.

Getting Started

Write the two following situations on a piece of paper and assign half your group one situation and half the other.

SITUATION 1

You have been hit by a car and are now paralyzed from the neck down for life.

1. Do you want to see your friends or would you rather be left alone?

2. What activity would you miss most?

3. Realistically, how many friends do you think would stick with you if this really happened? Which ones?

SITUATION 2

A good friend has been hit by a car and is paralyzed for life from the neck down.

1. Do you think you would still hang out with this friend?

2. What would you do and say if you went to visit him or her?

3. Would you invite your friend out if you knew you would have to push his or her wheelchair?

Looking in the Word

While sitting on the roof, ask your students to read the passage and then retell what they have read from the vantage point of the characters. Assign each student one: the friends, the paralyzed man, the owner of the house, the Pharisee.

Plugging into Daily Life

Ask:

1. If you want to bring your friend to the Lord, what qualities of friendship do you think it would be important to have?

2. What are some practical ways that people are introduced to the concept of Christianity?

3. Why do you think some Christians are reluctant to discuss Christianity with their unbelieving friends?

Adding It All Up

Ask your students to think of one non-Christian friend. Take a moment to silently pray for wisdom about how to introduce that friend to Jesus Christ.

ON-SITE IN A GARDEN

Take your students to a garden or orchard to teach a lesson about the agonizing night Christ spent in Gethsemane.

> **Focus:** God suffered in our place.
> **Bible passage to share and discuss:** Matthew 26:36–46.

Getting Started

Ask how many of your students have ever fallen asleep during class, church services, or some important function. Explain to your students that they are not alone. Christ's followers fell asleep during one of his most trying and difficult times.

Looking in the Word

While in the garden, ask your students to read the passage of Scripture and come up with an excuse that the disciples might have given for their behavior that night.

If your students can handle it, ask some tough questions about the passage:

1. What did Jesus mean by praying, "May this cup be taken from me"?

2. Why would Jesus pray that kind of prayer?

3. What does this incident tell you about the nature of Christ?

4. What was Christ's attitude in facing pending difficulties?

Plugging into Daily Life

Randomly distribute copies of the following assignments, writing them on slips of paper:

1. What are some tough situations that could be faced by a student your age? Come up with a list of them. What should be your attitude during these tough times?

2. How do Christians (or the Christian community as a whole) "sleep" during important crisis times? Give some illustrations.

Ask your students to share what they have written.

Adding It All Up

Invite your students to pick one flower or leaf from the garden and press it in the pages of their Bible as a reminder of Christ's suffering in Gethsemane.

Take your students to a local cemetery and teach your lesson while sitting on or around a grave site.

Scout out beforehand the best location to teach from. Try to find a grave of a person who died at a fairly young age to give more gravity to the lesson.

While there are a number of lessons that can be taught in a cemetery, death seems to be the common denominator of all of them. The recent death of a local student or of a well-known individual will heighten the impact.

Variations: Go to the grave of a person known to most of the students (such as one of the church elders) and talk about his or her life, and the people he or she touched in a godly way during their time on earth. Or go to the grave of an infant and talk about tough subjects such as why small children suffer and die. Abortion is another sensitive subject that could be discussed in this manner.

Focus: The reality of death and the promise of eternal life.

Bible passages to share and discuss: Psalm 103:14–16, Isaiah 25:8, Luke 20:34–38, 1 Thessalonians 4:13.

Getting Started

After your students have seated themselves around the site, ask for a show of hands to the following question:

"How many of you think about death— Do you think about it a lot? Seldom?

Never?"

Point out that regardless of how often they think about death, it's almost impossible to avoid considering it while sitting in a cemetery.

Looking in the Word

Read or distribute Scriptures that you've chosen to use. Ask each student to select one passage that they could put into their own words. Ask several to share the passage they have personally paraphrased.

Plugging into Daily Life

Involve your students in a discussion about the differences between philosophies that have no hope and the Christian faith. Ask questions such as:

1. How should a life be lived if death were the final experience?

2. How would you conduct your life if you thought you would merely die, like a plant or an animal?

3. Do you think it is wrong for a Christian to be afraid of death? Why or why not?

4. Why do you think people act so casually about death when they know that they too will die?

Adding It All Up

Ask your class to take individual walks through the cemetery. They are to quietly think about their own inevitable death, to weigh their own preparation and priorities.

Ask them to think about what kind of epitaph they might want on their grave to give people who wander through the cemetery a bit of hope for eternal life. If they are equipped with pencils and paper, have them write their epitaphs at the cemetery. If not, have them write them when they get back to the meeting place.

TREE

Sitting in the branches of a large strong tree is a perfect way to bring home to your students the story of Zacchaeus, the tax collector.

Naturally, you'll want to choose a tree that will sustain the weight of your class. Bring a ladder with you to help the kids who are not part monkey.

Being up in a tree will limit what you can hold in your hand or work on. The best idea is to so familiarize yourself with the Scripture that you can simply tell the story while sitting in the tree.

A tree isn't the cleanest environment. Warn your students before the trip to wear clothing for the outdoors.

Focus: Jesus comes to us while we are still sinners.
Bible passage to share and discuss: Luke 19:1–10.

Getting Started

After you're securely lodged up in the tree ask your students to describe to the group the best seats for an event (such as sports or concert) that they have ever had. Tie that into the lesson by saying that a seat similar to the ones you now occupy was the best seat that a guy named Zacchaeus could get when he tried to see the event of the year in Jericho: Jesus coming to town.

Looking in the Word

In the tree, retell the story of Zacchaeus and his encounter with Christ. Do a little background investigation so that you can explain the significance of a tax collector to the Jewish people. Prepare some discussion questions. For example:

1. What would be your response if a total stranger invited himself to dinner at your house?

2. What indications did Zacchaeus give that he had genuinely changed his way?

3. Why did the people mutter against Jesus eating with Zacchaeus?

Plugging into Daily Life

Ask your students to discuss:

1. What are modern equivalents of tax collectors?

2. What do you think shows that we have a genuine faith in Christ?

3. What should our actions and attitude be toward today's "tax collectors"?

4. Do you think people who become Christians should make some sort of restitution to people they've cheated before they were Christians? Why or Why not?

Adding It All Up

Ask your class to spend a few moments in silent prayer for a friend who doesn't know about Christ. Have them ask God to give them an opportunity to show them the depth of their faith by their kind deeds and actions.

Taking your kids to a pigpen for this lesson on the Prodigal Son may not be the most pleasant experience in their lives, but it will make this a lesson they won't soon forget.

Because of the stench in a typical pigpen, you may want to stay just long enough to get your point across and then continue your lesson somewhere else. Or surprise your students by beginning work on the prodigal parable in the classroom and then taking them to see a pigpen first hand when you reach the part of the passage that tells of it.

Focus: The parable of the prodigal son.
Bible passage to share and discuss: Luke 15:11–32.

Getting Started

Involve your students in a discussion about leaving home, perhaps using these questions:

1. Did you ever try to run away from home when you were a little kid? What happened?

2. What's the youngest age at which a person is ready to leave home? Why?

3. Consider this situation: a typical eighteen-year-old is leaving home for the first time and wants access to a trust fund that had been set up for him by a relative. Should he get it all, part of it, or none until he has proved himself? Why?

Looking in the Word

Before leaving the pigpen, have your students look up Luke 15:11–32 and read the passage. Then have students (individually or in small groups) divide the passage into scenes. (For example, one scene would be a young man who has decided to leave home.) Retell the story of the Prodigal in cartoon strip form using each scene as a panel in the cartoon. Have your students write in thought balloons for the Prodigal Son that show what he might have been thinking at each stage of the game. Have the students leave blank the panel in which he dines with pigs. Visit the pigpen, and then have your students complete the pigpen panel of their cartoon.

Plugging into Daily Life

At the pigpen start a discussion about the results of straying from God's provision and authority, using these questions:

    1. What do you think hanging out with the pigs might have signified to Christ's Jewish audience?

    2. What parallel do you think a pigpen could have in our society today?

    3. Is there a message in this parable for those who want to lead their lives however they choose?

    4. What can you do to make sure you don't end up in the pigpen of life?

Adding It All Up

Ask your students to come up with a motto that they might be able to use to keep them from ever having to "learn the hard way" like the Prodigal Son.

NARROW PATH

To bring home the concept of the singularity and narrowness of the way of salvation, find a narrow passageway from which to teach your lesson. The best sites are those thin gullies or passageways caused by water erosion.

The path should be too narrow to accommodate more than one student at a time, but not so tight that it would be a fat man's misery.

If the site requires a hike, you may want to make a day event of it and bring along a lunch.

Focus: Jesus is the Narrow Way.

Bible passages to share and discuss: John 14:6, Matthew 7:13–14, Luke 13:24.

Getting Started

Ask your students to offer their opinions of the following statement: Most non-Christians think it's pretty easy to *get to heaven*. When they've discussed it, offer the observation that public opinion does not always reflect reality.

Looking in the Word

Read or pass out reproductions of the Scripture passages to your students jammed in the narrow way. Ask them to suggest words that describe the limitations or pressures of squeezing through a narrow path.

Plugging into Daily Life

Stimulate a discussion about the narrowness of the Christian teaching by asking questions such as:

1. What would you say to a person who complains that the teachings of Christ are too exclusive or narrow?

2. What does this teaching say to a person who believes that every path sooner or later leads to God?

3. What does the experience in the narrow way tell you about people who want to bring their worldly baggage (ideas, values, possessions) with them into Christianity?

Adding It All Up

Ask your students to prayerfully consider whether they are actually following the narrow path of Christianity. Give them some time of silent prayer to consider how well they are following the path.

COURTROOM

Acourtroom is a great place to bring to life the idea of God as judge. The difficulty is to actually get into a courtroom. They aren't always available to the public, or if they are, the schedule may not coincide with the schedule of your meeting. The best way to acquire the use of a courtroom is to have an inside "connection" such as a judge, who will work with you to clear the paperwork and get your class inside.

Focus: God is a just Judge.

Bible passages to share and discuss: Malachi 3:5, Acts 17:31, Romans 2:2–16, 2 Peter 2:9.

Getting Started

Work with your class through the courtroom and show your students (many who will never have been in a courtroom before) the place where witnesses sit, where the judge sits, where the defense sits, and so on. Mention that this courtroom is an earthly imitation of the great courtroom where God will judge men's souls.

Looking in the Word

Divide your students into two groups: lawyers for the defense and lawyers for the prosecution. Distribute the Scripture passages to each group and have them create a case for three individuals:

1. A person who wanted to have nothing to do with God.
2. A native from some remote jungle

tribe who has never heard of Christ but tried to love the great god of his people he had heard of with all his heart and to do good.

3. A Christian who was a murderer before his or her conversion, but now was trying to love God.

Have your students bring their cases before you as the judge.

Plugging into Daily Life

Provoke a discussion about God's justice by asking questions such as:

1. Do you think God needs to be fair and just by human standards? Why or why not?

2. What rules do you think God goes by?

3. Do you think it's fair to judge someone by his thoughts and motives as well as by his actions? Do you think this is what God will do?

Adding It All Up

Ask your students to write one sentence that they could use in their defense when they stand before the Living God. Have them share what they have written.

BARN, SILO, OR WAREHOUSE

O ne of these locations will help bring to life the parable that Christ told about the rich fool—to show the folly of the accumulation of "things" (which was the main goal of the rich fool), and the additional foolishness of not investing in heavenly treasure.

These sites tend to be messy: warn your students to wear clothes that they don't mind getting dirty.

Focus: We must be rich in our love for God.
Bible passage to share and discuss: Luke 12:13–21.

Getting Started

Ask your students to give their opinion on the question: "How much is too much?" (or, "How much material goods should be considered an excess?") After they've shared their thoughts, introduce the parable that you will be looking at today.

Another way to get started: Ask the students to try to guess the value of the products stored there. Try to get an accurate estimate from the owner beforehand. See which student comes closest.

Looking in the Word

Have your students read the parable and then identify the crucial mistake that the rich fool made. Ask them to share where they think he got off track.

Plugging into Daily Life

Distribute paper to your students and ask them to write a modern version of this parable, using an example other than a barn and crops. Have them share their ideas.

Adding It All Up

Ask your students to come up with a list of ideas that would help a person invest in heavenly rather than earthly treasure.

Ask each person to select one thing from that list to do this week.

WHEAT FIELD

Harvest, fruit bearing, and soil are frequent images in the parables and metaphors of Scripture. What better way than a visit to a wheat field (especially for city kids) to bring home the concepts that Jesus taught using wheat as a metaphor. For instance, Jesus used wheat and chaff to symbolize the difference between genuine believers and the insincere.

An alternative lesson from a wheat field could deal with Christ's vicarious death (see John 12:24).

It can strengthen your lesson if you are able to time your visit when the wheat is in full bloom and if you can arrange to harvest and winnow a bit of it.

Focus: God will separate those who truly believe from those who do not.

Bible passage to share and discuss: Matthew 3:11–12, 13:25–30.

Getting Started

Take your class out into the field and harvest a small bundle of wheat. (Ask beforehand for a grower's help in knowing where to cut the stalk and how to winnow.)

Discuss what the differences might be between a well maintained and cultivated field and a field that was hand cultivated and tilled.

Looking in the Word

Read to your students the passages of Scripture that you have chosen to use. Ask them to find in the wheat samples of weeds or chaff. Ask them questions such as:

1. What does wheat signify in the scripture?

2. What do weeds or chaff signify?

3. Who separates the weeds from the wheat?

4. What happens to the weeds and chaff? What does this signify?

Let your students try to separate the wheat from the chaff with the old method: winnowing with a piece of cloth and the wind.

Plugging into Daily Life

Weeds and chaff symbolize sin and phoniness. Ask your students to give some suggestions of the kind of weeds and chaff that might be found in a typical youth group.

Adding It All Up

Ask each of your students to contribute a sentence sharing something that God may say to a believer (and possibly to them) through the parable of the wheat field.

ON-SITE AT A MANURE PILE

Some lesson sites make their impact by involving one of the senses far more than others. This lesson is one of those.

Paul wrote that he compared all of the great things that he had accomplished to rubbish—or, in the original language, "dung"—when put next to gaining Christ. This lesson can be poignantly brought home by visiting a manure pile at the local dairy or cattle feed lot.

Obviously, you won't want to make your visit to the manure pile last any longer than necessary to get the point across. Even so, your students won't forget this lesson for a long time.

Note: This on-site activity works best if you can keep your location secret until the last minute.

Focus: There is nothing that even comes close to knowing Christ.

Bible passage to share and discuss: Philippians 3:4–9

Getting Started

Involve your students in a discussion about status, fame, power, and the rewards that come with it. Ask questions such as:

1. If you could be anything you wanted, what would it be? Why did you pick that?

2. Do you think that there is really anything special about a president, rock star, or actress? If so, what? If not, why do you think people are so easily impressed by them?

3. Can you think of anyone in the Bible who could brag because of his or her credentials?

Looking in the Word

Just before arriving at the manure pile review with your students what Paul had to say in Philippians 3:4–9. Explain that Paul was using rather graphic language to emphasize the vast difference in value between what he had given up and what he had gained. At this point, pull up to the manure pile.

It won't take too long on-site for your students to get the point.

Plugging into Daily Life

After you've left the manure pile, discuss with your students the things that kids their age think are more important than knowing and growing in Christ. Ask:

1. If people really loved God, would they no longer try and educate themselves or would they refrain from taking jobs of importance? Why or why not?

2. What should be our attitude about our achievements?

3. What are three of the biggest competitors for a Christian's allegiance?

Adding It All Up

Ask your students to write a prayer to God asking his help in making their spiritual relationship the most important thing in their lives.

I f you live near the coast chances are there is a lighthouse (active or inactive) nearby that will make a perfect backdrop for a discussion on the importance of a Christian's example to the non-Christian community and the need to tell others about Christ.

It works best to conduct your lesson in the tower of the lighthouse. But even sitting on the grounds of the lighthouse brings home the lesson.

Make your lesson more interesting by doing a little research into the history of the lighthouse and of any shipwrecks nearby.

Focus: Christians must let others see Christ by their actions and words.
Bible passage to share and discuss: Matthew 5:14–16.

Getting Started

Let your students roam around the grounds and check out the cliffs, the structure, and so on. Call them together and tell them something of the history of the lighthouse you are visiting.

Looking in the Word

Share the passages of Scripture with your students and involve them in a discussion by asking questions such as:

1. What are the similarities between the job of this lighthouse and the job of a Christian?

2. Where does the power to light up a person come from?

3. What happens if a Christian has a "power outage" or runs inconsistently?

Plugging into Daily Life

Ask your students to list as many ways as possible to let our light as Christians shine in a high school setting. Ask them to list actions that will impede the light's shining.

Adding It All Up

Distribute index cards and a pencil to each student and ask them all to write down the name of one friend who is heading toward the rocks of life. Have them write one thing they could do this week that would serve to illumine this person's life. Have your students take the cards home as a reminder to be a light for Christ.

ON-SITE IN A SYNAGOGUE

For something unique and informative try taking your students to a Jewish synagogue. If possible, have the rabbi talk to your students about things like the bar mitzvah, Passover, the Torah, and other aspects of the Jewish faith that are historically linked with Christianity. (You may be surprised at how many rabbis are willing to do this for you.)

Obviously, you will want to inform your students that this is not a debate opportunity but a chance to be informed about important ideas from the Bible.

It can be great fun too!

Focus: To get a better understanding of some important biblical practices.
Bible passage to share and discuss: Luke 2:21–35

Getting Started

Before your visit, give the rabbi who will show you around the synagogue an idea of what subjects and questions you'd like him to address.

Tell your students your destination. Discuss rules of conduct, and a brief background of what Jews believe about Christ.

Looking in the Word

Have your students review the passage of Christ being presented at the temple. Create a list of questions about that ceremony and any other questions about Jewish practices—either those from the Bible or those which are practiced today.

Visit the synagogue. Ask your students to take notes on what the rabbi will share.

Plugging into Daily Life

After your visit, take some time to ask your students for their impressions and questions.

Adding It All Up

Have your students create a thank-you card for the rabbi who helped you. As a group, pick several Jewish people to begin praying for regularly.

HOUSE OF MIRRORS

A fun house that has a number of distorted mirrors is a great place for some creative learning. The mirrors offer distorted views of reality, just as the world's wisdom does. Contrast those mirrors with an accurate one like God's Word, and you have the seeds for a great lesson.

A house of mirrors is also a good place for kids to use their creativity to find biblical applications themselves, and have fun doing it.

Focus: God's Word is the perfect picture of truth.

Bible passage to share and discuss: James 1:22–25.

Getting Started

On your way to the house of mirrors, ask your students how many times in a day they look in a mirror.

Looking in the Word

Before entering the house of mirrors have your students examine the passage from James. Note the difference between God's perfect Word and the distortion that the world produces as truth.

Have your students locate the key idea in this passage.

Plugging into Daily Life

Assign each student the task of creating an image in one of the mirrors that corresponds to some distortion in the world. For example, an image with a swelled head represents people who think too much of themselves. Take a picture of each student demonstrating their distortion. (An instant camera works best.)

Have your students write an appropriate caption to explain each picture.

Adding It All Up

In advance, prepare enough blank bookmarks so that each student will have one.

Remind your students of how often they peer into a mirror each day. Ask them how many times in a day, week, or month they look into the mirror of their souls—the Bible.

Distribute the bookmarks and encourage your students to write down the key passage from James on their bookmark as a reminder to reflect often in the pages of the Bible.

SPRING

A springhead flowing out of the ground can be used to better communicate the idea of Christ being "Living Water." If the only spring you can find requires a long hike, you may want to have your students put a lunch in a day pack and make an outing of your lesson.

It's great if you're lucky enough to find a spring that your kids can drink freely from after their hike.

As with all activities that involve water, plan for wetness.

If there's no spring nearby, see whether you can locate a well of some sort to gather around.

Focus: Christ is our Living Water.
Bible passage to share and discuss: John 4:1–26.

Getting Started

If the spring's water is drinkable, let your students satisfy their thirst. Then, while sitting around the spring, ask your students to think of as many names for Christ as they can. Sooner or later someone is bound to come up with "Living Water." Let them know that this is the idea you have come to consider today.

Looking in the Word

Read or tell the incident of Jesus and the woman at the well. Spark a discussion by asking:

1. Why do you think Jesus used figurative language when describing a spiritual idea? Do you think this is helpful or confusing? Why?

2. What are the symbolic similarities

between God and the element of water?

3. What message can be drawn from Christ's willingness to talk to a person of another culture and religion?

Plugging into Daily Life

Ask your students to suggest things that people may use to try to satisfy their thirst. Discuss the end result of each of the substitutes suggested.

Discuss ways that Christians will often block the "Living Water" from flowing in their lives.

Adding It All Up

Create a circle of prayer with your students and invite each of them to pray for God to better flow through them or for some friends who need to have their thirst satisfied.

With a little cooperation from a bank manager, you may be able to get your group into a bank vault for at least a part of your lesson.

The best bank to ask for this favor may be the one your church does business with.

A bank vault is a great place to discuss protection, the security of God or any lesson having to do with money.

You may want to have the manager explain to the students how a bank vault works, since most of them will never have been inside of a vault before.

As with other lessons where pulling a favor, be sure to write a thank-you note after the lesson.

Focus: We should invest our treasure in permanent things.
Bible passage to share and discuss: Mark 10:17–27.

Getting Started

Ask your students to name the largest amount of money they've ever held in their hands. Ask:
1. How did you feel holding so much cash?
2. Where did you get it?
3. What did you do with it?

Looking in the Word

After your tour of the bank vault, sit your students down and have them read the story of the rich young ruler.

Have half of your class write an editorial column that takes sides with the rejected young ruler. The other half can write an editorial that supports what Christ did. Discuss the editorials.

Plugging into Daily Life

Discuss whether it's possible for any of us to possess something more valuable than God. Ask your students to retell the story of the rich young ruler but to substitute some other "love" that the person won't give up to follow Christ. (For example, Jesus meets a real party animal.)

Adding It All Up

Ask your students to create a "hazardous" label like the warning on the side of tobacco products that might be placed in bank vaults or printed on money, identifying the clear dangers of making money a god.

VINEYARD

ON-SITE IN A

Taking your group to a vineyard can give them a lasting picture of a number of Christ's parables and teachings.

Try to arrange your visit a vineyard while the grapes are still on the vine. The farmer may be willing to come with you into the field and explain the pruning process.

If there are no commercial vineyards in your area, check with people in the church. Someone may be growing grapes in their backyard.

> **Focus:** We must stick to Christ in order for our lives to bear fruit.
> **Bible passage to share and discuss:** John 15:1–17.

Getting Started

At the vineyard, let your group feast on grapes from the vine, if you have permission. Discuss the idea that Jesus used grapes, vines, and branches in many of his teachings.

Looking in the Word

Assign each student a portion of John 15 to read; then ask them to prepare a several-sentence summary in their own words.

Ask students to interpret what they think Christ means by a vine, a branch, fruit, pruning.

While we know that this teaching was directed primarily at Israel, ask your students to explain in their words the point Jesus is trying to make to his followers today.

Plugging into Daily Life

Ask your students to suggest practical ways a Christian can maintain a good relationship with Christ.

Adding It All Up

Ask each of your students to write down something they learned about vineyards, God, or our connection to him from today's lesson.

ON-SITE AT A

POLLUTED POND

This is a lesson on purity. From the banks of a pond or river that is full of waste you can demonstrate graphically the results of not filtering the pollutants of sin out of our lives. Any pond with brackish water, old tires, and rubbish will do. Unfortunately, there are many of these kind of ponds around. Scout out a setting in advance that will best fit your lesson. One possible service project as an offshoot of this lesson is to clean up the area with your youth group after the lesson.

Focus: God wants us to be pure.

Bible passages to share and discuss: 1 Timothy 5:22, Philippians 4:8, Matthew 5:8.

Getting Started

Bring a glass to your polluted pond and scoop up some scummy water. Ask whether any of your students would care for a drink. Ask:

1. How much money would it take for you to drink this glass of water?

2. What diseases might you catch if you did?

3. What would it take to make this water pure again?

Looking in the Word

Sit on the bank near the pond (unless it's too smelly to be near). Have several students read out loud the passages of Scripture you have chosen.

Ask your students to give you a definition of the word "pure." Begin a discussion about spiritual purity by asking questions such as:

1. Do you think people are more cautious about the impurities they put in their

bodies than the impurities they put in their minds?

2. What are some examples of impure things that we take into our mind regularly?

3. Which of those things are unavoidable, and which do you have to go looking for?

4. What effect do you think spiritually impure people have on those around them? On the church?

Plugging into Daily Life

Discuss ways to filter out spiritually destructive impurities. Ask such questions as:

1. Other than hiding in a monastery, what are some ways to deal with the impurities that we take into our minds?

2. Should a Christian stop listening to or viewing secular music, radio, TV, film, or video? Why or why not?

3. What guidelines would you give to new Christians to help them avoid polluting their spiritual lives?

Adding It All Up

Pass out index cards; have each student create a motto stating his intention to filter possible pollutants from his spiritual life.

ARMORED CAR

This is one *On-Site* activity that everyone looks forward to—especially junior highers: a lesson taught from the safety of an armored car.

To get the use of an armored car, it helps to have connections—but you might be surprised at what a simple request can accomplish. Keep in mind that a small group is much better for this activity.

If you can arrange it, have a driver cruise you around town while you teach your lesson.

If you live near a military base, you might be able to get permission to use a mothballed tank or personnel carrier. Both would work well for this activity. Talk to the base commander or chaplain.

Focus: God is our shield against Satan's attack.

Bible passages to share and discuss: Ephesians 6:16, Psalm 5:12, 18:30, 33:20, 84:11.

Getting Started

Have your host explain to you the workings of the armored car, what it will protect against, and how thick the walls and glass are. Encourage your students to ask questions.

Looking in the Word

Distribute printed copies of the passages of Scripture you want to use to each student. Ask them to draw comparisons between the armored car and the verses of Scripture:

1. Do you feel safer in this vehicle than in a regular car?
2. What does God keep us safe from?
3. What might we do that would jeopardize God's protection?

Plugging into Daily Life

Have each of your students take one of the verses and personalize it with his or her name and an incident from life. For example, Psalm 5:12 might sound like: "For surely, O Lord, you will bless John if he is righteous, you will surround him with your favor during times of disappointment for not making the team as you would with a shield."

Have your kids share their rewritten verses with each other.

Adding It All Up

Ask your students to create a jingle for an ad slogan that would represent the protection that God offers those who seek him.

ON-SITE IN A

CANCER WARD

Certain kinds of realities are hard for the average kid to grasp—especially in the area of godly priorities or values. Most of the people in this world have their priorities backwards. Often, it takes a brush with death to make a person reevaluate what is important. Taking kids to a cancer clinic can help spark that reevaluation.

Consider combining your lesson with some sort of service project in the hospital. Ask the nurses for ideas; they often know what would be the most welcome. Obviously, you'll need to clear your plans with hospital officials.

Be sure to explain to your students what type of behavior you expect from them. Ask them to try to put themselves in the place of the patients.

If you can't take your students into the hospital itself, just sitting on the grass outside the hospital can still have an impact.

Focus: We must bring our priorities in line with God's way of thinking.
Bible passages to share and discuss: Matthew 6:33, Hebrews 9:27.

Getting Started

Before leaving for your destination (and before you have informed your students where you are going) ask your group, "If you just had a physical examination and the doctor said 'There is something I need to talk to you about,' what would be your greatest fear?" Their responses may be wide and varied, but very likely someone will mention a disease that has the potential to be terminal. When they've completed their responses, explain where you're going and the purpose of the lesson.

Looking in the Word

Begin your lesson by sharing the idea that many people, when faced with a potentially fatal illness, reevaluate what is really important in life. Have your students examine the passages you select and then create a list of priorities in life that are dictated by Scripture.

Plugging into Daily Life

Ask your students to help create a double list: on one side, what people usually live for and what they might live for if they were faced with pending disaster. Contrast the values represented in the two columns.

Adding It All Up

Ask your students to imagine that they were diagnosed as having cancer, and that they knew they had only a short while to live. Have them write letters to their friends and families, expressing what would be important to them if they really faced imminent death.

ON-SITE AT A FISH POND

Sometimes combining fun and a lesson can help create a connection to Scripture that will never be forgotten. One way to do this is to create a lesson about being "fishers of men" combined with a fishing trip.

Of course, you will need to bring bait, fishing poles , clean equipment, and a charcoal grill (if you plan on eating your catch). Kids can learn a lot from the comparisons of winning a fish for supper and winning another person to faith in the Lord!

Focus: God wants us to actively win others to Christ
Bible passage to share and discuss: Mark 1:14–20.

Getting Started

At the fishing hole discuss what kind of fish you're going after and what kind of bait they like. Show kids how to bait their hook and to cast without scaring away the fish.

Looking in the Word

Distribute preprinted copies of the Scripture to all of your students. Ask them to memorize verses 16–18 as they sit waiting for a fish to bite.

Plugging into Daily Life

As you wrap up your short fishing trip ask your students:

1. If we are to be "fishers of men" what kind of "bait" do you think would be attractive to people who don't know Christ?

2. What is the significance of Andrew and Simon Peter leaving their nets behind to follow Christ?

3. What things of our old life might we have to leave behind when we decide to become "fishers of men"?

4. What would you say is the single most important way to effectively be a witness for Christ in a school like yours?

Adding It All Up

Ask students to think of one friend that they know who is not a Christian. Ask them to consider an action that they could take this week that would make coming to Christ more interesting to this person. Close by having each student silently pray for the person they have thought of.

OLD FOLKS' HOME

This lesson can be combined with a service project directed to the senior citizens in your community or to people in retirement homes or convalescent hospitals.

With the exception of Grandma and Grandpa, many kids seldom get a chance to interact with people of the oldest generation. Putting kids in contact with old people (especially those who are still vital) can teach them a valuable lesson in respect, compassion, understanding, and dignity. The Bible clearly teaches that old people have a wealth of wisdom and experience to learn from.

Note: If your group is to visit people who are sick, handicapped, or very weak, it may be good to take an older person with you who is in the peak of health, so that kids can see that old age is not automatically the same as incapacitation.

Focus: Old people have great worth, value and wisdom

Bible passages to share and discuss: Job 12:12, Proverbs 16:31, Psalm 92:12–15.

Getting Started

Ask:

1. How old would you like to live to?

2. What is something that do you do now that you plan to still be able to do when you are eighty?

3. What do you find most interesting about old people?

Looking in the Word

Ask your students to read the passage and then to help you create a list of attributes that come with a life of godly living.

Ask: What kind of treatment do you think the Bible suggests for older people?

Plugging into Daily Life

With your students create "ten commandments" we should consider in order to show respect to old folks and a willingness to learn from them. Hang your ten commandments on the wall of your classroom.

Adding It All Up

Distribute pencils, paper, envelopes, and stamps to your students. Ask each of them to write a letter to an old person they know, asking for advice and insight on a number of issues. (You may wish to brainstorm some issues with the students before distributing the paper.)

BAKERY

Some ideas in Scripture are difficult for students to visualize, especially ideas that are tied in with a custom no longer practiced within view of the ordinary kid. One such idea is Christ's teaching about the leaven or yeast of the Pharisees. Most of today's kids have no idea of what leaven was (or is). They think bread magically shows up at the grocery store each night.

A great way to bring this teaching to life is to show kids around a bakery so that they can watch bread in preparation. (It's especially nice if you can acquire some warm bread or donuts as part of the event.)

Focus: Don't be a hypocrite or a phony.
Bible passage to share or discuss: Matthew 16:5–12, Luke 12:1–2.

Getting Started

Ask your students whether they can define "leaven." If they can't, ask them to explain what "yeast" is. (Yeast is a fungi used in fermentation or baking.)

Looking in the Word

Provide each student with a clipboard, pencil, and paper. Before visiting the bakery, ask them to read the passage assigned and to write down in their own words what they think Jesus was saying.

Plugging into Daily Life

After the visit, ask your students, "Since Jesus warns us not to be involved in the same kind of sin as the Pharisees, can you come up with a number of areas where Christians might practice hypocrisy?" Write down what your students suggest.

Adding It All Up

Ask your students to identify at least one area from the list you have created in which they may be prone to hypocrisy. Have a time of silent prayer to ask God's help in strengthening those areas.

NURSERY

In this activity, you don't even have to leave the grounds of the church to get your point across.

Using the church nursery instead of the regular classroom, you can teach a vivid lesson on childhood.

The Bible uses childhood as a metaphor in a number of ways—such as being "babes in Christ" (meaning new or immature believers), having a childlike faith, or even being a child of God. Exploring through those concepts in a nursery is easy, because most nurseries come equipped with all the toys, books, and puzzles of childhood, which can be used in some part of your lesson.

Focus: We must have the faith of a child.
Biblical passages to share and discuss: Mark 10:15, Matthew 18:2-6.

Getting Started

Start by having a contest between a couple of kids to see who can put together a kiddie puzzle the fastest. Use this as a springboard to point out that as we get older we often leave all our childhood behind, but that God wants us to retain it in one area: our trust of Him.

Looking in the Word

Have your students read the passage. Working with crayons, have them restate the Scripture in words that a child of four might be able to understand.

Plugging into Daily Life

At least a day or two before the lesson, spray paint a child's puzzle white. Pass out at least one piece of the puzzle to each student, along with marking pens. Ask each student to list on his or her piece of puzzle one childlike attribute Christians should try to copy in their faith, as well as one thing that God can be counted on to do as our Father and one responsibility we have toward our brothers and sisters in Christ.

Put the puzzle back together.

Adding It All Up

Close your class by singing "Jesus Loves Me" together.

One vivid way to illustrate the difference between spiritual light and spiritual darkness is to take your students to a very dark room (which you may have to prepare in advance) and conduct your lesson in the dark.

Naturally, control can be a problem when you can't see who is doing what. But even this can be used to demonstrate that we often behave differently in the dark than we would in the light.

Switching on a powerful flashlight at appropriate times during the lesson makes the contrast become more dramatic.

Obviously, you'll need to study your text before taking the kids into a dark room. Any paperwork will have to be done before or after going on-site.

Focus: Jesus is the Light for a dark world.
Bible passages to share and discuss: John 1:4–9, 3:19–21, 8:12, 9:5, 12:35–36.

Getting Started

Involve your students in a discussion about childhood fears of the dark. Ask questions like:

1. How many of you were afraid of the dark?

2. What did you think lived in the darkness?

3. Where do you think you got those ideas?

4. Are you still afraid of the dark?

5. Would any of you walk by yourself through a cemetery in the dark?

Looking in the Word

Assign each person in your class a passage or two to read. Ask them to write a question about the verse they have been assigned and then pass the paper to another person in the group.

After each has come up with a response to the question they were given, have them share the questions and the answers.

Plugging into Daily Life

Take your students to a dark room and initiate a discussion about the darkness of sin by asking questions such as:

1. What similarities between the condition of this room and the condition of a person's heart without Christ?

2. What limitations does darkness put on a person? What limitations does sin put on a person?

3. If you lived in this kind of darkness for a month straight do you think you would be happy with your appearance if the lights suddenly came on? Why or why not? What would be the parallel to this idea in the spiritual realm?

Adding It All Up

Distribute candles to each student, explaining that we as Christians do not have to live in darkness. Light a match, and as you light each candle ask your students to say a silent prayer thanking God for bringing his light into their lives.

To bring a new dimension to the Lord's Supper, try taking your class to an upper room all set up for dining.

The closer you can come to the original scene the better. Try having the kids sit on the floor around a low table, wash each other's feet, and have a genuine meal celebrating Christ's death for us.

Focus: Christ shed his blood to pay for our sins.

Bible passages to share or discuss: John 13:1–17, Luke 22:7–22.

Getting Started

Well in advance of your lesson, find an attic, a loft, or some other "upper room" that you can bring a class to.

About a week before your lesson, send out invitations to all your students, giving them the time and location of the class at the upper room. (Be sure to post the information on the door of your classroom at church in case anyone shows up who is not on your mailing list.)

Have the room set up in advance, and the elements waiting for your group members when they get there.

Try having your students remove their shoes and socks before they enter the room; then, before they are seated, wash each of your students' feet.

Try to keep a solemn atmosphere and say as little as possible to your students as you perform the foot washing. (Note: the reaction of your group to foot washing can vary, but most kids catch on pretty quickly if the environment is sober and serious.)

After your students have been seated, ask them how they felt about having their feet washed.

Looking in the Word

Divide your chosen passage of Scripture into short, readable sections; assign those sections to several members of the class who are strong readers. Let them take turns reading to the whole class.

Ask your students to describe what the disciples might have been feeling and thinking during the Last Supper.

Plugging into Daily Life

Distribute slips of paper and ask your students to write down a sin that they have committed this week that Christ's blood removed. Ask them to tear up the paper to signify their confession and repentance of the sin and God's faithfulness to forgive it.

Adding It All Up

Close your lesson by having your students celebrate the Lord's Supper together. But make it a real meal as the early church did. Sing a hymn or praise song and then dismiss.

POTTER'S WORKSHOP

I n the Bible, God is often portrayed as the Master Potter and humans as lumps of clay to be molded and shaped by his hand. Vessels of clay were also used to represent the temporary and delicate nature of our physical bodies. In fact, clay is almost synonymous with being human, from our creation to the destruction of our physical body.

A visit to a potter will give your students a peek back in time as well as a chance to realize the potential in a mere lump of clay such as ourselves. The doctrine of God's sovereignty can also be communicated in this lesson. But be forewarned: this study may raise some tough questions. Be prepared to deal with them.

Arrange in advance for the potter to put on a demonstration for your students. If possible, let your students attempt to use the wheel themselves.

Focus: God molds us and makes us like He wants.

Bible passage to share and discuss: Romans 9:14–21.

Getting Started

Bring a few lumps of kiddie clay to class with you. Tell your students that they have a few minutes to make the clay into the best object they can.

After they've finished (and you have had a good laugh at their creations), inform them that they're going to see how a real pro works with clay.

Looking in the Word

Ask your students to read the assigned passage and then to define the word "sovereign." Then leave for the potter's workshop.

Plugging into Daily Life

After you've seen the potter's demonstration and your students have tried their hand at the potter's wheel, initiate discussion about God's supreme power by asking:

1. What do you think the idea of God as the Master Potter says to those who call themselves "self-made men"?

2. What attitude should we have toward the way that God made us?

3. What should we do if we don't like the way we have been created?

Adding It All Up

Give each student a piece of clay or pottery to take home as a reminder that God is in charge of his or her life. If you distribute shards of fired pottery, ask your class to write down a key verse from the passage in Romans on their piece of pottery. Close in prayer.

FIELD

The parable of the sower and the seeds is often taught in the average church. Make it come alive by dragging your kids to places that parallel the teaching in Scripture.

Most fields or gardens will work for this activity. Find representative areas of the four types of soil in advance, and then guide the students to them—or you can send the kids out to locate examples of each type of soil (and even bring specimens back in small containers).

Of course, the parable of the sower and the seeds is not the only teaching that can be drawn from a field. There are plenty of important biblical ideas that use harvests, fields and fruit-bearing as their metaphor.

Focus: Our souls are like gardens that can be either fertile or barren.

Bible passage to share or discuss: Luke 8:1–15.

Getting Started

Ask your students how many of them have ever grown a little garden. Ask those who have to tell about it. You will probably find many who have a black thumb for growing things.

Load your kids up for a trip to the field.

Looking in the Word

Have your students read the parable of the sower. Assign each person in your group the job of locating a particular kind of soil as described in the parable. Distribute shovels and buckets if you wish students to bring their samples back with them.

Plugging into Daily Life

Involve your students in a discussion on the meaning of the parable for Christians today by asking:

    1. Which of the seeds do you think was truly saved? Why?

    2. What are some weeds in our daily life?

    3. What does it mean to "not have root in ourselves"?

    4. How does Satan steal the word—the "seed"—away from us?

Adding It All Up

Ask each student to return to the field and find a weed that could represent some hazard to spiritual growth in his or her life. Ask them to keep the weed as a reminder of what to watch for in their own day-to-day lives.

ON-SITE ON

CENTER STAGE

Center stage, being *in the spotlight*—both refer to the idea of being the prime attraction, something that most of us want in our unregenerated pride. Of course, the Christian idea is just the opposite: We are to avoid putting ourselves at the center of attention and instead give the glory to God and to others.

While center stage is not wrong in a theatrical sense, it can be deadly when it becomes our focus for living.

To pull off this lesson, you'll need a stage area and, if possible, a spotlight. (You can create your own with a high-powered flashlight.)

Focus: God wants us to seek the welfare of others, not our own glorification.

Bible passage to share and discuss: Philippians 2:3–8.

Getting Started

Have all of your students sit in the center of the stage area. Ask them to describe what they think of when they see someone who's obviously in love with his own sense of importance. Point out the connection between being the center of the action (center stage) and having an overinflated idea of your own importance.

Looking in the Word

Ask your students to read the passage of Scripture and then write a note from God, the chief director, to one of his actors with instructions regarding sharing the spotlight.

Plugging into Daily Life

Ask your students to brainstorm several ways to put others ahead of themselves at:
School
Church
Home
Athletic Activities
Write down what they contribute and take it back to class with you.

Adding It All Up

Ask each student to write a prayer to God asking to be kept humble and for help in thinking of others as more important than themselves.

FOUNDATION

Take your students to the foundation of a new building or home for a visible lesson on Christ as our foundation and cornerstone.

Take along a broom in case the site is littered with construction debris and you need to sweep an area to sit down on.

If the building under construction has a cornerstone, point it out to your students.

Focus: God is the One whom we build our lives upon.
Bible passage to share or discuss: Matthew 7:24–27.

Getting Started

At the site, start a discussion about the need for a foundation. Ask:

1. What would happen if they tried to put up this building without the foundation?

2. What would cause someone to try to build a building without a foundation?

Looking in the Word

Go over the parable of the wise and foolish builders with the students. Ask:

1. How can you be sure you're building your house on the rock, or foundation?

2. What do you think rains, streams, and winds represent?

3. What are some of the ways in which people build their lives on the sand?

Distribute paper and clipboards to your students and have them draw a cartoon strip about a builder who ignores the blueprints and builds his house anywhere he pleases.

Plugging into Daily Life

Ask your class to come up with a list of excuses people give as to why they don't build their lives on Christ. Then, ask them to come up with a response to each excuse.

Adding It All Up

Give your students a short, "quiet time" to consider whether the heavenly building inspector would approve the foundation that their own lives are being built upon.

The Bible often uses sheep as a metaphor. What better way to drive that imagery home than to do some actual shepherding? If your students aren't familiar with sheep, they will probably be amused to think that God often compared us with these slightly dense animals.

The best way to observe these animals is by watching their behavior in a herd on the open field. If this isn't possible, just having your group hang around a few sheep in a barnyard will help drive home the biblical concepts.

Let your students know in advance what to wear if you plan on doing the barnyard shuffle.

Focus: God wants to be our leader, guide, and shepherd.
Bible passages to share and discuss: Matthew 9:36, 10:6, 18:11–13, John 10:1–5, Psalm 23.

Getting Started

Give each of your students a note pad and pencil and send them out to observe and record everything they can about sheep in a predetermined amount of time. Share results.

Looking in the Word

Assign students portions of Scripture to read and rephrase in their own words. Have your students create a dialogue that might take place between a sheep who wants to go looking around and a sheep who knows he should stay near the shepherd. Encourage them to look for the benefits and pitfalls of each position.

Plugging into Daily Life

Discuss the similarities between sheep and people. Ask questions such as:

1. In what ways do people stray from the safety of God?

2. What are some ways that people are attacked by the "wolf"?

3. Why is it important that the Shepherd "calls us by name"?

4. What traits did you observe in the sheep that might be similar to human traits?

Adding It All Up

As a group, create a sheep's pledge to follow and obey the commands of the Great Shepherd.

ON-SITE AT THE

BEACH

A beach or lakeshore can serve as a launching pad for a number of ideas. God's power is revealed in the rolling waves. The promises of God to Abraham are represented by trying to count a few million grains of sand. (Try counting them!) You could discuss the parable of the builders, then build sand castles and watch them be destroyed by waves. Or, you could use the site to discuss a biblical incident that happened on the shoreline—such as Christ's breakfast on the beach with his disciples.

It is probably best to visit a portion of beach that has few or no people. As with any event scheduled near water, expect that most, if not all of your students are going to get wet and have them prepare for the possibility.

Focus: Reenact Christ's breakfast on the beach.
Bible passage to share and discuss: John 21.

Getting Started

Ahead of time, send out announcements to all of your class that you will be having breakfast for disciples of Christ at the beach instead of your regularly scheduled class. Make sure to give time, date, and location.

When the kids arrive, have breakfast ready.

Looking in the Word

Read or retell the events in John 21 to your students. Make sure to point out the hesitancy of Peter's response to Jesus when asked if he loved the Lord. (In the original language, Peter used the word *friendship* rather than the word *love*.)

Plugging into Daily Life

Ask your group, as followers of Christ, what kind of responsibilities they think Christ has given them. Discuss their response.

Adding It All Up

Give your group a chance to reaffirm their own discipleship; let them move apart individually for a few minutes for a time of personal prayer and private meditation with God.

ON-SITE AT A FORTRESS

Depending on where you live, you may be able to find an old fortress, bulwark, or the remains of some fortification. (Most of these are national parks or monuments.) Even an old World War II pillbox can work as a place for this lesson. These sites are excellent places to give a lesson about God being our place of refuge.

Before teaching your lesson, study about the fort, you'll be going to and read up on the method of laying siege to a fortress in Bible times. (This information can be found in a good Bible commentary and in historical works available in libraries or Christian bookstores.)

You might not want to teach your lesson in the fort itself, (especially if it is crawling with tourists). You might just want to take your students to a nearby park after you tour the fortress and complete your lesson there.

Focus: God is our hiding place.

Bible passages to share and discuss: Psalm 9:9, 18:2, 59:9, and 16, 61:3, 91:2, Proverbs 14:26.

Getting Started

Summarize for your students the history of the particular fortification that you're visiting. Explain to them the similarities between this kind of fortification and the walled cities of the Bible.

Looking in the Word

After you have visited the fortress, review the passages of Scripture with your class. Have each student pick out a verse he thinks best expresses the idea of God being our place of refuge.

Plugging into Daily Life

Ask your students to brainstorm a list of times when a Christian would especially want to take refuge in the protection of God (or would be grateful for that protection).

Ask:

1. Do you think it shows weakness to take refuge in God? Why or why not?

2. Is it fair to ask God to protect us from the results of our wrongdoing? Why or why not?

Adding It All Up

Read to your students the words to the hymn "A Mighty Fortress is Our God" (or sing the song together). Encourage each student to memorize the verse that seemS most significant to him or her.

ON-SITE
40 ON-LOCATION YOUTH PROGRAMS

Are your young people growing tired of the same old youth meetings and Sunday School classes?

Then hold your next youth meeting . . .

    AT A GARBAGE DUMP
    IN A JAIL
    AT A CEMETERY
    IN A BOAT
    AT A BAKERY
    IN A TREE
    ON A ROOFTOP

. . . or at any one of the 40 "On-Site" locations found in this book! Break the boredom cycle by teaching the Bible while visiting places like a dump, a beach, a pig pen, a garden, a vineyard, a warehouse, a hospital, even a bank vault!

Even though **ON-SITE** is a new idea in Christian education curriculum, it's really an old idea. Jesus used the same technique. He taught people on location and drew upon His surroundings for living object lessons: "Consider the lilies of the field . . ."

ON-SITE activities are creative "field trips" that provide a wide variety of experiences and lessons for the young people in your church. They will learn better and remember more when they are "on site" using their senses of sight, sound, smell, and touch to discover the truth of the scriptures.

Inside this book are 40 complete lesson plans which include a tri⸻⸻⸻⸻ **ON-SITE** for special Sunday School classes, junior high or high scho⸻⸻⸻⸻ you want to give your young people a break from the usual classroom ⸻⸻⸻

Rick Bundschuh is a writer, cartoonist and youth minister living in Hawaii. He was formerly the editor of youth curriculum for Gospel Light Publications. He has authored several books for youth, including GLOW IN THE DARK and SHADOW OF A MAN.

ISBN 0-310-43061-5

9 780310 430612

a ZONDERVAN PUBLICATION

10822p
YOUTH SPECIALTIES
YOUTH MINISTRY
ISBN 0-310-43061-5